Dear Parent:
Your child's love of reading starts here!

Every child learns to read in a different way and at his or her own speed. You can help your young reader improve and become more confident by encouraging his or her own interests and abilities. You can also guide your child's spiritual development by reading stories with biblical values and Bible stories, like I Can Read! books published by Zonderkidz. From books your child reads with you to the first books he or she reads alone, there are I Can Read! books for every stage of reading:

SHARED READING
Basic language, word repetition, and whimsical illustrations, ideal for sharing with your emergent reader.

BEGINNING READING
Short sentences, familiar words, and simple concepts for children eager to read on their own.

READING WITH HELP
Engaging stories, longer sentences, and language play for developing readers.

READING ALONE
Complex plots, challenging vocabulary, and high-interest topics for the independent reader.

ADVANCED READING
Short paragraphs, chapters, and exciting themes for the perfect bridge to chapter books.

I Can Read! books have introduced children to the joy of reading since 1957. Featuring award-winning authors and illustrators and a fabulous cast of beloved characters, I Can Read! books set the standard for beginning readers.

A lifetime of discovery begins with the magical words **"I Can Read!"**

Visit www.icanread.com for information on enriching your child's reading experience.
Visit www.zonderkidz.com for more Zonderkidz I Can Read! titles.

"Let there be more and more birds on the earth."

—*Genesis 1:22*

ZONDERKIDZ

Our Feathered Friends
Copyright © 2011 by Zonderkidz

Requests for information should be addressed to:
Zonderkidz, *Grand Rapids, Michigan* 49530

Library of Congress Cataloging-in-Publication Data

Our feathered friends.
      p. cm. – (LCR standards. Level 2)
  ISBN 978-0-310-72184-0 (softcover)
  1. Birds–Religious aspects–Christianity–Juvenile literature.
BR115.B55O87 2011
231.7–dc22
                                                    2010016483

Editor: Mary Hassinger
Art direction & design: Jody Langley

Printed in China

13 14 15 /DSC/ 10 9 8 7 6 5 4 3 2

I Can Read!

••• MADE•BY•GOD •••

Our Feathered Friends

CONTENTS

God made everything,
and he made it all good.
He made bugs that crawl
under the dirt and birds that fly
way up high like the …

EAGLE!

There are about 59

kinds of eagles.

Some kinds of eagles are:

Bald eagle

Golden eagle

African fish eagle

Steppe eagle

Eagles are amazing birds.

Some have about 7,000 feathers!

Their wings can stretch out to be

as tall as the ceiling.

They have superstrong beaks

and claws to help them eat.

Eagles build nests of

sticks and twigs.

Some nests are huge—

up to ten feet across.

The eagles put their nests up

on cliffs or in trees to protect

their babies, called eaglets.

Eagles are called birds of prey.

That means they hunt for food.

Eagles like to eat mice, snakes,

and some even like to go fishing.

God put eagles all over the world.

They like to live in high places

and near water.

One special eagle, the bald eagle,

lives in the United States

and was named the

symbol of the USA in 1782!

God made the powerful eagle

and the tiny and gentle …

HUMMINGBIRD!

The hummingbird is amazing too. There are about 320 kinds of hummingbirds. Most of them live in the western half of the world. These tiny birds love warm weather.

The smallest bird that God made
is very special.
The hummingbird's heart beats
1,260 times every minute!
Its wings beat 53 times per second.
The wings make a humming sound.

Hummingbirds can hover,

fly backward, forward,

and even upside down.

While flying, hummingbirds

use a long, skinny beak

to eat nectar, sap, bugs, and spiders.

Hummingbirds are only three or
four inches long.

They weigh less than one ounce.

But hummingbirds eat
almost all the time.

God made these tiny,
quick-flying birds, and he
made the amazing and
quick-running …

ROADRUNNER!

When God created the roadrunner

he made them so they

could run 17 miles an hour!

They can fly, but they love to run.

Roadrunners live in the desert in southwest USA and Mexico. They have a long tail that sticks straight up.

Roadrunners are part of
the cuckoo bird family.
Roadrunners can grow to be
ten to twelve inches tall.
They weigh about one-
and-a-half pounds.

Roadrunners eat many things
like bugs, seeds, and fruits.
They can even run fast enough
to catch a rattlesnake to
eat it!

God made everything
and he made it all good.
He made birds that fly and
run all day,
and he made a bird that
loves the night.
It is the …

OWL!

Owls are nocturnal.

That means they move

around the most at night.

Owl eyes work best in the dark.

Owls are birds of prey
like the eagle.
Owls like to eat small birds
and animals, bugs, and reptiles.
Owls have sharp beaks and
strong claws to help them eat.

Owls can grow to be

20 to 28 inches tall.

Their wings can stretch out to be

four to five feet across.

Owls cannot move their eyes.

They turn their heads

all the way around to see!

They have special

feathers that help make them

silent when they fly.

God made more than 220
kinds of owls.

Some of them are:

Saw-Whet owl

Great gray owl (the biggest—
  33 inches tall)

Snowy owl

Barn owl

Great horned owl

God made everything,

and he made it all good.

Just look around and something

special might just fly by!